Citizenship

Being a Good Citizen

Adrian Vigliano

Raintree is an imprint of Capstone Global Library Limited, a company incorporated in England and Wales having its registered office at 7 Pilgrim Street, London, EC4V 6LB – Registered company number: 6695582

www.raintreepublishers.co.uk
myorders@raintreepublishers.co.uk

Edited by Rebecca Rissman, Siân Smith, Charlotte Guillain, and Vaarunika Dharmapala
Designed by Kimberly Miracle
Original illustrations © Capstone Global Library Ltd 2010
Illustrated by Mark Beech
Originated by Steve Walker, Capstone Global Library Ltd
Printed and bound in Dubai

ISBN 978-1-4062-8884-1 (paperback)
18 17 16 15 14
10 9 8 7 6 5 4 3 2 1

British Library Cataloguing in Publication Data
Vigliano, Adrian.
  Being a good citizen. -- (Acorn plus)
  1. Citizenship--Juvenile literature.
  I. Title II. Series
  323.6'5-dc22

We would like to thank Nancy Harris and Adriana Scalise for their invaluable help in the preparation of this book.

Every effort has been made to contact copyright holders of material reproduced in this book. Any omissions will be rectified in subsequent printings if notice is given to the publishers.

Contents

Some words are shown in bold, **like this**. They are explained in "Words to Know" on page 23.

What is a citizen?

A **citizen** is a member of a **community**. Communities are made up of the people around us.

There are many ways to be a good citizen. Do you know how to be a good citizen?

At school

When you follow the rules, you help make your school a **fair** place for everyone. How can you follow the rules at school?

You can raise your hand before speaking. You can ask before taking something. You can walk quietly down the hallway. You can wait for the teacher's **instructions.**

A **leader** is someone who takes charge and sets a good example. How can you be a good leader at school?

You can help others with a problem. You can invite others to join in. You can keep trying. You can **praise** others. You can give others a turn to lead.

At home

When you are helpful, you are thinking of ways to help others. You are also listening to others to learn what they need. How can you be helpful at home?

You can put away toys. You can do the washing up. You can help carry things. You can follow **instructions**. You can look out for others. You can ask what you can do to help.

When you are **responsible**, you take charge of what you do. When you are responsible, you do the right thing without being asked to. How can you be responsible?

You can brush your teeth or clean your room without being asked to. You can put on your seatbelt in the car. You can **admit** if you make a mistake.

With friends

You can be a good **citizen** while you are with friends. You can also be a good citizen by making new friends. Friends **trust** one another and have fun together. How can you make friends?

You can ask someone to play with you. You can **share** your things. You can tell someone you like them. You can listen to others. You can take turns. You can say sorry when you are wrong.

You can be a good friend by being **honest**. When you
are honest, you tell the truth and people can **trust**
you. How can you be honest with friends?

You can tell someone how you feel. You can return something that is not yours. You can tell someone you made a mistake. You can **admit** that you were wrong.

You can be a good friend by being **fair**. When you are fair, you think of other people and find ways to treat them well. How can you be fair with friends?

You can **share** a snack. You can wait your turn. You can give someone else a turn. You can let others choose what to play. You can think about how others feel.

Being a good citizen every day

There are many ways to be a good **citizen**.
You can find ways to be a good citizen in
different places.

You can find ways to be a good citizen with different people.

How can you be a good citizen?

No matter where you are, as a good **citizen** you can be **responsible** for what is going on around you. If you see something that doesn't seem right, you can say something!

You can be a good citizen in your **community** by being a thoughtful family member, classmate, friend, and neighbour.

You can look for ways to take care of the **environment**.

You can treat other people with kindness and **respect**.

Words to know

admit   tell something that you may be afraid to tell

citizen   member of the community

community   any group of people. A community can be small like a family, or large like a school.

environment   nature and the world around us

fair   agreeable for everyone

honest   always telling the truth

instruction   written or spoken list of how to do something

leader   someone who takes charge and sets a good example

praise   to tell someone you think they did well

respect   to value something or someone and treat them fairly

responsible   to take charge of yourself and to do the right thing wherever you are

share   to let someone else use what you have; to give someone else a part of what you have

trust   to believe in someone or something

Index

Note to parents and teachers

Before reading:

Tell children that people in a community are called citizens. Communities are made up of the people around us. Ask children if they know how to be good citizens. Create a concept map with the children. In the centre of the map write "Good Citizens," and around the centre fill in their ideas of how to be a good citizen. Guide them towards words such as *responsible, honest, shares,* and *follows the rules.*

After reading:

• Assign children a word from a book that relates to being a good citizen.
  Ask children to write and/or draw a picture that relates to their assigned word.
  Create a class book from all the work.

• Place children in small groups. Ask each group to create a sign. The sign should show ways to be a good citizen at school. After their posters are complete, walk small groups around the school and help the children to put up their signs.